The Sufficiency of CHRIST

Devotions from Colossians

TOM HINKLE

The Sufficiency of Christ: Devotions from Colossians

©2024 Tom Hinkle

All Rights Reserved

Scripture quotations are from the ESV® Bible (The Holy Bible, English Standard Version®), copyright © 2001 by Crossway Bibles, a publishing ministry of Good News Publishers. Used by permission. All rights reserved.

ISBN 978-1-955295-48-2

100 Manly Street
Greenville, South Carolina 29601
CourierPublishing.com

Published in the United States of America

Dedication

I dedicate this book to the glory and honor of God the Father, Jesus, His Son and our Savior, and to the Spirit who guides us. The English Standard Version (ESV) has been used for the texts.

I am thankful for the support of my loving and devoted wife. I am grateful to those who have encouraged me in my walk with the Lord.

Introduction

Colossians is one of the four epistles written while Paul was in a Roman prison. The epistle focuses on the person and work of Jesus Christ.

Colossae was a city in the Roman province of Asia and formed a triangle with Hierapolis and Laodicea. It had once been a center of trade but by the first century was less in importance than the other two cities.

The Christian community was the outgrowth of the three-year ministry of Paul in Ephesus. The church at Colossae apparently grew up under the leadership of Epaphras and Archippus. Philemon and Onesimus lived at Colossae. Paul had heard of their faith from Epaphras, who had come to Rome to see Paul. Some new doctrines were creating problems in the church, and Paul wrote in order to refute those doctrines. The new doctrines were man-made philosophy based on traditions and not on divine truth.

Colossians gives us a firm foundation for the lordship of Jesus Christ. Paul wanted the disciples at Colossae to know that Jesus alone was the Supreme Lord and Savior of mankind.

The Sufficiency of CHRIST

Devotions from Colossians

Chapter One

Greetings

Paul, an apostle of Christ Jesus by the will of God, and Timothy our brother, to the saints and faithful brothers in Christ at Colossae: Grace to you and peace from God our Father. (1:1-2)

PAUL INTRODUCES himself to the readers as an apostle of Christ Jesus, by the will of God. Paul had been sent by God to be a messenger of the gospel. He is telling them that God gave him this authority and that Timothy has been his helper in this mission. He calls the believers at Colossae brothers in Christ. They have heard and believed the gospel and have been brought into the church that Jesus is building. Paul wishes them the grace and peace that God the Father gives to His children.

Since Paul had never been to Colossae, the believers there were unfamiliar to him. Epaphras had come to Rome to seek Paul's help in combatting the false doctrines that had come into Colossae. Paul wants the readers to know that what he is writing is not his own ideas but the instruction he has received from Jesus. He is glad to call them his brothers in Christ and wants to be able to help them be at peace with God. His hope is that he can help them know more about Jesus and how Jesus can help them as they grow in their faith.

*— Thank You, Father, for giving us Your Word —
that helps us learn to walk in the Spirit.*

> *We always thank God, the Father of our Lord Jesus Christ, when we pray for you, since we heard of your faith in Christ Jesus and of your love that you have for all the saints, because of the hope that is laid up for you in heaven ... (1:3-5a)*

ALTHOUGH PAUL had never been to Colossae, he wanted the believers to know that he prayed for them. He states he has prayed for them ever since he heard of their faith in Jesus and of their love for all saints. He wants them to know that the faith they have in Christ is the reason for their hope that is laid up for them in heaven. Paul has been informed about the false teachings that have come into Colossae and how some are saying Jesus is not sufficient to save. Paul assures the believers that when they trusted in Jesus, He was able to save them and keep them.

As Paul continues with his letter, he is going to make it clear that Jesus is all we need for salvation. In our day, there are many false teachings that try to add to the work of Christ for salvation. The Bible is clear: We are saved by grace alone through faith alone in Christ alone. Paul's letter will help us come to a better understanding of these truths. The believers in Colossae were in danger of being led astray by the teachings of the false teachers. Paul prays for them and writes to help them come to a better understanding of the person and work of Jesus Christ.

*— Father, help us to know that all we need —
is in Christ, Your Son and our Savior.*

The Colossians Had Heard the Gospel

Of this you have heard before in the word of truth, the gospel, which has come to you, as indeed in the whole world it is bearing fruit and increasing — as it also does among you, since the day you heard it and understood the grace of God in truth ... (1:5b-6)

PAUL SAYS the hope that the believers have is because they have heard and received the gospel. It is the gospel of Christ that is able to bring real hope to anyone who receives it. Paul states that the gospel is bearing fruit (bringing salvation) to the whole world. God has ordained that, through the preaching of the gospel, those who accept the truth of forgiveness can receive the hope of everlasting life. The people in Colossae had heard and understood the grace of God. They had therefore a basis for the hope that they were in a right relationship with God.

Only the saved are in a right relationship with God. God has sent His Son, Jesus, to be our Savior and Lord. When we are confronted with the truth that we are sinners and the only way to be made right with God is by accepting the death of Jesus as our payment for our sin, we then can call upon the Lord and be saved. God is gracious and gives us that call to come to Him for salvation. The believers in Colossae had come to understand this truth. We are saved by the grace of God through faith in Jesus Christ. That is the only way to be saved, and we need to make that clear to those we know.

— Thank You, Lord Jesus, for saving me. —

> *...just as you learned it from Epaphras our beloved fellow servant. He is a faithful minister of Christ on your behalf and has made known to us your love in the Spirit. (1:7-8)*

PAUL HAD not been to Colossae, but the church had been founded by a Colossian named Epaphras, who apparently had been saved while Paul was preaching in Ephesus. Epaphras had come to Rome to seek help for the church. Some teachers had come in and were causing divisions in the church. Epaphras stayed with Paul and prayed with him for the churches of the Lycus Valley, Colossae, Hierapolis and Laodicea. Epaphras was faithful in his preaching and teaching the gospel of Christ. Paul commended him for this and told the church that Epaphras had told him of their love for Paul. No doubt Epaphras had shared with them the importance of Paul's missionary work.

As Paul writes to the Colossians, he reminds them of the work of Epaphras, who had been faithful in bringing them the gospel. Paul wants them to understand that all they need they have in Christ. Whatever the false doctrines were, there seems to be an attack on the completeness of the work of Christ and the person of Jesus. Many were confused and may have been following some of these teachers who were not being true to the gospel of Christ. Today, many want to add to the work of Jesus and refuse to accept salvation by the grace of God by faith alone in Christ alone.

— *May I be faithful to preach the truth of the gospel.* —

And so, from the day we heard, we have not ceased to pray for you, asking that you may be filled with the knowledge of his will in all spiritual wisdom and understanding, so as to walk in a manner worthy of the Lord, fully pleasing to him, bearing fruit in every good work and increasing in the knowledge of God. (1:9-10)

PAUL SHOWS his concern for the church by telling them that he is praying for them. That fact must have encouraged the believers. Just as today when someone tells us they are praying for us, these believers had to appreciate that Paul was praying for them. His prayer was that they would be filled with the knowledge of God's will in all spiritual wisdom and understanding. Often, we may think we know God's will but may not understand all we want to understand. God gives us guidance through the Spirit and His Word. We can know God's will and understand that He is leading us, even though we may not understand all the circumstances.

Paul had told the Roman believers that all things work together for good to those who love God and are called according to His purpose. Now he tells the Colossians that they can be filled with the knowledge of God's will. They have the Spirit to guide them into all truth. By walking in the Spirit, they can be pleasing to God. God will guide them and give them an increase in the knowledge of His will. God will help them as they seek to do good works to His glory.

— To God be the glory for all His goodness to us. —

> *May you be strengthened with all power, according to his glorious might, for all endurance and patience with joy, giving thanks to the Father, who has qualified you to share in the inheritance of the saints in light. (1:11-12)*

PAUL WANTS the believers to understand that God the Father has given them power to endure and have patience. The false teachers may have been trying to persuade them that God could not help them at times. They were to be careful how they stood for the truth they said they believed. Paul wants them to understand that no power in this world or the next can take a child of God out of the hand of God. We are saved and secure in Jesus. The Colossians had been accepted by the Father because of their faith in Jesus. Jesus had promised the disciples He would never leave them or forsake them. That promise is true for all believers. We may try to leave God, but He will never leave us.

Many false teachers have tried to say that a saved person can lose his salvation. One of my deacons used to say if you are truly saved you can never be lost again. That, I think, is what Paul is trying to convey to the Colossians. If they will remember what Jesus did for them, they will be assured of His continual care of them. As Dr. John Rice used to say, if you got saved by something you did, you can lose that; but if you got saved by what Jesus did, you can never lose that. Knowing Jesus will help us to be full of assurance by His grace.

— *May I teach others to fully trust in Jesus.* —

> *He has delivered us from the domain of darkness and transferred us to the kingdom of his beloved Son, in whom we have redemption, the forgiveness of sins. (1:13-14)*

PAUL TELLS the believers at Colossae that they have been delivered from the domain of darkness. The Bible pictures the world as being under the control of the Prince of Darkness, Satan. That darkness causes all people to be blind to the truth of the gospel and the love of God. Paul says when we come to Jesus, He delivers us from darkness into the light of the gospel. God opens our eyes spiritually and we can see to come to Him. We come into the kingdom of God's beloved Son and receive the forgiveness of our sins.

Since it is sin that separated us from God, it is good news that we can receive the forgiveness of sins. That gospel truth is what the devil wants us never to hear. God is willing and able to deliver us from the domain of darkness and bring us into the kingdom of His beloved Son. When we come to faith in Jesus, we can receive the forgiveness of our sins and can become a child of God. This is the work of God by His grace that allows us to hear the gospel and believe it and come to Jesus. Now Paul emphasizes that when we come to Jesus, we are redeemed. Our sins are paid for, and we are now free from the penalty of sin. We can have, by God's grace, God's power to resist sin, and someday we will be with Jesus and be free from the presence of sin.

— *Thank You, Father for saving me with the gospel.* —

> *He is the image of the invisible God, the*
> *firstborn of all creation. (1:15)*

PAUL NOW begins to speak about the supremacy of Jesus. Paul wants his readers to worship the Son of God. Paul had no trouble telling his readers that Jesus was God. Even though God the Father is invisible, God the Son became a man and we beheld His glory. Paul had met Jesus on the road to Damascus, and he knew firsthand the reality of Jesus as the Son of God. The invisible God came as a man and lived among us so that we could be brought back to God. Paul's statement that Jesus is the firstborn of all creation is not saying that Jesus was a created being. Paul is using the idea of Jesus as the firstborn to emphasize His supremacy and authority. Jesus, the Son of God, has always existed with God the Father and God the Spirit. He became a man in obedience to the Father to bring salvation to His people.

We may ask, what does God look like? We cannot see God; He is invisible. We do not know what Jesus looked like when He became a man and walked among us. But we need to understand God did become a man — His name was Jesus. He came to show us the Father and to reveal to us the hope of eternal life. The resurrected Jesus was the first fruits of those who sleep. Having been included in His death, we shall also be in His resurrection. Paul wants us to know that God has done all that needs to be done in His Son to bring us salvation and eternal life. We shall live forever because Jesus is alive.

— Thank You, Father for the blessed hope we have in Jesus. —

For by him all things were created, in heaven and on earth, visible and invisible, whether thrones or dominions or rulers or authorities — all things were created through him and for him. (1:16)

PAUL CONTINUES to tell of the nature of Christ as the supreme God of the universe. John, in his gospel, asserts all things were made by Him, and without Him nothing was made. From the Genesis account, we see that all three persons of the Trinity were involved in creation. Paul now states that Jesus has authority because He was a part of the creative process. The purpose for creation was for God to have man made in His image to fellowship with Him. When man sinned and turned from God, it did not surprise God. He had already made a plan for our redemption. God's Son was ordained before the foundation of the world to be our sacrifice. Hence, Paul can say that all things were made *by* Jesus and *for* Jesus.

There are many today who do not believe the Genesis account of creation. But God's Word says, "In the beginning, God created the heavens and the earth." That is what Paul is affirming here. The problem many have with the Genesis account is they don't believe in an all-powerful God. He spoke all things into existence. Some in Colossae were doubting the reality of Jesus and His power. Paul points them back to creation to show the authority and power of Jesus.

*— The heavens and the earth declare the glory —
of the Lord. Help me to remember that fact.*

And he is before all things, and in him
all things hold together. (1:17)

PAUL WANTS to set the record straight. He has already warned the readers at Rome that many were worshiping the creation more than the creator. That may have been a part of the false teachings that were causing trouble at Colossae. Jesus was before all things. Paul is stating that it is because of Jesus that all things hold together. As we have studied the universe and all that is in it, we are amazed at some of what we call the laws of nature. God's order of this world is fascinating. The more we discover in our universe, the more we realize how little we really know. And yet, Paul writing under the guidance of the Spirit tells us all things were made by God and all things hold together because of God. That is why the Bible says the man who says there is no God is a fool.

Many today want to believe in an account of creation that leaves God out. But the only reliable record of creation is the Genesis account. Some scientists today talk about a creative force but don't like to say it is God. Paul does not hesitate to say that God created the world. If we look around us, we are amazed at the complex nature of our world. It only makes sense that someone more powerful and wiser than man had to bring this into existence. Some want to talk about the Big Bang Theory. I saw a bumper sticker that I liked. It said: "I believe in the big bang theory; God spoke, and, *bang*, it happened."

— *To God be the glory for all His creation.* —

> *And he is the head of the body, the church. He is the beginning, the firstborn from the dead, that in everything he might be preeminent. (1:18)*

PAUL STATES strongly that Jesus is the head of the church. Maybe there had been some dispute among the believers at Colossae, but Paul wants them to know that Jesus is the head of the church. Paul points out that the death, burial and resurrection of Jesus proved Him to be the Son of God. Not only was Jesus resurrected, but He gives the promise that we also will be resurrected with Him. Paul tells us that Jesus is to be preeminent in everything. There is no other name given among men whereby we can be saved. Some had brought false teaching about other ways to God. Jesus declared, "I am the way to the Father." When God raised Jesus from the dead, He placed His approval on the death of Jesus as payment for our sin.

We need to share with others who Jesus is. He is the Son of God and the Savior of all those who believe in Him. God did not have to save us, but in His mercy and grace He sent His Son to redeem us. Paul says Jesus is the head of the church and we are all members of His body. Jesus is to be lifted up so that all men might be drawn to Him. There is no one more important to the salvation of mankind than Jesus. Many false teachers want to take away the position of Jesus, but He is the Sovereign Lord, Creator and Sustainer of mankind.

— Thank You, God, for sending Your Son to save us. —

> *For in him all the fullness of God was pleased to dwell, and through him to reconcile to himself all things, whether on earth or in heaven, making peace by the blood of his cross. (1:19-20)*

PAUL CONTINUES to explain who Jesus was and is. He is God in the flesh. The incarnation means that God became a man. The mystery of the incarnation is that Jesus was 100 percent God and 100 percent man in one person. He did not give up His deity to become a man. And Paul states the reason that Jesus came was to dwell with us and to reconcile all things to Himself. Paul had told the Corinthian church that God was in Christ, reconciling the world to Himself. Christ was able by His death, burial and resurrection to reconcile all things in earth and heaven to God. He brought peace to God and man through the blood of His Cross.

It is hard for us to fully understand the incarnation. God coming to us in the form of man may confuse us. We may wonder why it was necessary for Jesus, the Son of God to take on a human form. The Bible explains that since we were separated from God by the sin of a man, we had to be reconciled by the obedience of a man. Jesus, because He was sinless, could be the sacrifice for our sin. God put our sin on Him and imputed His righteousness to us. That is the good news of the gospel. We can be made right with God by receiving God's free gift to us of forgiveness of sin because of the payment of Jesus.

— Praise God for His unspeakable gift: salvation. —

And you, who once were alienated and hostile in mind, doing evil deeds, he has now reconciled in his body of flesh by his death, in order to present you holy and blameless and above reproach before him … (1:21-22)

PAUL SPEAKS of the believers as having been alienated and hostile in mind. He is making sure that they understand that they had no claim to God and His goodness. They were doing evil deeds. We are not sinners because we sin; we sin because we are sinners. We are born with a nature contrary to God. Sin separates us from God and from each other. God was willing to make a way for us to come back to Him. He sent Jesus, who now reconciles us in His body of flesh by His death. God gives us forgiveness because Jesus was willing to pay our sin debt. We were unable to pay for our sin, but God made the payment by giving the life of His Son to reconcile us to Himself.

Paul tells the believers that Jesus reconciled them so that He could present them holy and blameless and above reproach to God. That is the condition that every born-again child of God is in. We are reconciled to God and presented holy, blameless and above reproach in Christ. But all of the benefits we have come to us because we are in Christ. As the hymn says, "Nothing in my hand I bring, simply to thy cross I cling." As a sinner, I could not make myself righteous before God. But, by the grace of God, I can have faith in the finished work of Christ and be reconciled to God. I am saved.

— Thank God for saving me and bringing me to Himself. —

> *... if indeed you continue in the faith, stable and steadfast,*
> *not shifting from the hope of the gospel that you heard,*
> *which has been proclaimed in all creation under heaven,*
> *and of which I, Paul, became a minister. (1:23)*

PAUL NOW brings the readers to an important point. If they continue in the faith, they have a choice: They can believe what Paul tells them, or they can listen to the false teachers. We are not sure what the false teachers were expounding, but it seems to be a message that tries to add to the work of Christ for salvation. Dr. Johnny Hunt said, "If there is a fall before the finish, there was a flaw in the first." Dr. John Rice used to say, "If you got saved by the blood of Jesus, you can never lose that salvation." Paul tells his readers to be stable and steadfast. He warns them not to shift from the hope of the gospel they had heard. Paul says the gospel has been proclaimed in all creation, and he has become a minister of that gospel.

Sometimes you may hear someone say, "I hope I can hold on until the end." We don't have to hold on because we are not holding on to Him — He is holding on to us. The work that God has begun in us, He will complete. The gospel is the good news that God is willing and able to save us. God gave His Son to be the satisfaction for our sin. We have passed from death unto life by the work of Jesus. Being born-again, we are born unto a living hope.

— May I rest in the finished work of Jesus to save me. —

> *Now I rejoice in my sufferings for your sake, and in my flesh I am filling up what is lacking in Christ's afflictions for the sake of his body, that is, the church ... (1:24)*

PAUL STATES that he rejoices because in his flesh he is filling up what is lacking in Christ's sufferings. He is not saying that he is adding something to the work of Christ by suffering. But he is stating that all who follow Christ will suffer. Jesus told us, "In this world you will have tribulations, but be of good cheer; I have overcome the world." Paul is saying, "I am a minister of Christ's, and so I will be willing to suffer for the sake of the church." Paul wants the believers at Colossae to know that even though he is in jail, he still has the joy of Jesus in his life. His concern is for them and wants them to remain faithful to the gospel.

It sounds strange to us to have someone say, "I rejoice in my sufferings." That is because we know very little about suffering for the cause of Christ. In many parts of our world there is physical threat if you are a Christian. That is how it was in the first century. Paul suffered much for his preaching of the gospel. As he is writing this letter, he is in prison. Perhaps we miss many blessings because we do not have to suffer as Paul did. Paul says, "When I am weak, then I am strong." May God help us to recognize our weaknesses so that we can ask for and receive His strength. As we walk with Jesus, He will provide the strength we need and His joy.

— Thank You, Jesus, for being with me in all my — circumstances. I want Your strength and joy with me.

> *... of which I became a minister according to the stewardship from God that was given to me for you, to make the word of God fully known, the mystery hidden for ages and generations but now revealed to his saints. (1:25-26)*

PAUL STATES that his ministry is a stewardship from God. God had placed him in the position of responsibility that he had. He was given the opportunity to make the word of God fully known. Paul, a devoted student of the Old Testament, was able to explain the truths of God that had been mysterious in the past. He states that this mystery had been hidden for ages and generations, but now God had made it clear. The truth about the Messiah had been revealed in the life and ministry of Jesus. Paul had been made an apostle to tell the good news of the gospel of Christ. What God had done in Christ was the full revelation of God's dealings with Israel and the world. We can have a relationship with God through the finished work of Jesus. Our sin can be forgiven and cleansed.

Paul makes it clear that the task of the minister is to make the Word of God fully known. So often, people say they don't understand the Bible. There is a lot in the Bible that is still a mystery. But the truth is: What we need to know is clear. We are sinners and separated from God. Sin brings death that is eternal. But Jesus died to pay for our sin and give us eternal life. That is the good news Paul was sharing, and so should we.

*— Help me, Lord, to be a faithful witness to the saving —
work that You provide for those who will believe.*

> *To them God chose to make known how great among the Gentiles are the riches of the glory of this mystery, which is Christ in you, the hope of glory. (1:27)*

PAUL SHARES with the Colossians that God has given him the responsibility of telling them the mystery of God's love for them. God has chosen to make known His riches of glory to the Gentiles. The hope that they have is theirs because they have received Christ. He now lives in them, and they are a part of the family of God. There is no other way to come to God than through Christ. Whatever doctrines the false teachers had been teaching, Paul states they are indeed false and are not needed. As Christians, we have all that we need to be right with God when we receive Jesus as our Savior and Lord. Paul is trying to make sure his readers understand the sufficiency of Christ. Salvation is by grace alone, through faith alone in Christ alone.

God had chosen and used Israel to bring blessings to the whole world. The plan of God led Him to send His Son to redeem people from sin. While the Old Testament has clues about what is going to happen; it isn't until Jesus comes and lives among us and becomes our payment for sin that we are aware of all that God had planned. Paul states that the mystery of God has been revealed in Jesus. We can now be made right with God because God has accepted the death of Jesus as payment for sin. We can be forgiven because we have received new life in Christ.

— *Thank You, Father, for the forgiveness of sin.* —

> *Him we proclaim, warning everyone and teaching everyone with all wisdom, that we may present everyone mature in Christ. (1:28)*

PAUL HAS just written: "Christ in you the hope of glory"; now he states, "It is Christ that we proclaim." We warn and teach everyone with the wisdom of God. Our goal is to present everyone as mature in Christ. Paul not only wanted people to believe in Jesus, but he wanted them to grow up in Christ. As Christians, we have the Holy Spirit and the Word of God to help us learn the things of God. We are to grow in the grace and knowledge of the Lord. Paul says that he did all he could to help the believers be more complete (mature) in Christ. Salvation is a wonderful event in our lives, and growing in Christ helps us to appreciate Jesus all the more. By proclaiming Jesus and all that He had done for sinners, Paul was able to help them come to salvation. Being saved is wonderful, but it is so much better if we will continue to grow in our faith.

As Christians, it is our responsibility to proclaim the good news of the gospel. Some are called to preach, but all are called to be witnesses. As we teach and warn others, we can help them come to a knowledge of Jesus Christ as Savior and Lord. Then we should seek to help new believers grow in Christ. How sad when we sometimes forget to help new believers, and they become confused and may even be led away from the truth.

— Father, help me be faithful in proclaiming Jesus. —

For this I toil, struggling with all his energy that he powerfully works within me. (1:29)

PAUL WANTED his readers to know that he was working as hard as he could — but it was not really Paul working, but God working in and through him. He says, "The energy that I have is being powerfully supplied by God as He works to do His good pleasure in me." This may have been the reason that Paul was so tirelessly working. He knew that God was suppling the energy and that God would not fail to see him through. All the trials that Paul endured helped him to know that God was with him. Paul knew that God had seen him through many hardships and that God would continue to supply the help that he needed. Paul knew that "when I am weak, then I am strong." The strength that Paul relied on was not his but the Lord's.

One of the problems we face as Christians is discouragement. If we are not careful, we get anxiety and worry about our walk with the Lord. Too often, it is because we have forgotten that we are not to work in our strength but in the power of the Lord. We will fail in our strength, but in the power of the Lord we can continue to walk with Him. We may feel like things are not going well, but we cannot trust our feelings. We walk by faith, not by sight. What we think we see may not be at all what is really going on. God promises to never leave us and to carry us through any situation. May we learn to trust and obey as we follow the Lord.

— Thank You, Lord, for giving me Your power. —

Chapter Two

For I want you to know how great a struggle I have for you and for those at Laodicea and for all who have not seen me face to face ... (2:1)

PAUL HAD never been to the church at Colossae or the church at Laodicea, but he was writing to let them know how he was working for them in prayer. He was concerned that these churches be strong in the Lord. Epaphras, who was probably a convert of Paul at Ephesus, had started the work in Colossae, and many believe also in Laodicea. Although Paul had not been to either church, he was concerned about their well-being. He states that he is struggling greatly. This does not mean that he was overwhelmed but that he was working as God guided him to help them. He would ask that this letter be read to the church at Laodicea. Paul felt a great responsibility for those who received the gospel that they not be led astray by false teachers.

We are not sure what false teachings had come into the church at Colossae, but Paul wanted to warn them against accepting any doctrine that tried to replace Jesus as the supreme Lord. He pictured this as a struggle because he was constantly having to defend the faith. We must defend the true gospel. Jesus was and is the Son of God. He was virgin-born, lived a sinless life, and died for our sin. We must defend the truths of the gospel as Paul did.

— Help me to be true to the gospel of Christ. —

> *... that their hearts may be encouraged, being knit together in love, to reach all the riches of full assurance of understanding and the knowledge of God's mystery, which is Christ, in whom are hidden all the treasures of wisdom and knowledge. (2:2-3)*

PAUL IS writing to encourage the believers so that they can come to a full assurance of the knowledge of God's mystery. The mystery is revealed in Christ. All that God had been doing was brought to full revelation when He sent His Son. Jesus was not just a man; He was the God-man. God took on a human form, and His name is Jesus. All the riches of God have been given to us who have received Jesus as Savior and Lord. From before the beginning of time, God had a plan to redeem His creation. The Godhead had met, and the Son accepted the Father's request to be the sacrifice for sin. The Holy Spirit had guided men as they wrote and helped to unveil the mystery through time until Jesus came.

Paul states that, in Christ, all the treasures of wisdom and knowledge are hidden. Jesus showed Himself to be God by His miracles and His resurrection. All that we need to know about God and His love for us is revealed in Jesus. He was made wisdom for us. In Him all the fulness of the Godhead dwells. Paul wants to encourage the believers to learn about Jesus. The hymn writer wrote: "He's all I need." That is what Paul wants to get across to his readers. Jesus is the one and only Supreme Lord and Savior.

— All praise to the King of kings and Lord of lords. —

*I say this in order that no one may delude
you with plausible arguments. (2:4)*

PAUL WANTED the church to know about his concern for them. Although we do not know what false teachings had come into the church, they concerned Paul. There were many different doctrines that the Jews and Judaizers tried to use to either turn people away from Jesus, as the Jews did — or to bring them under some practices of the Mosaic law, as the Judaizers did. Paul states some of these arguments may seem to be plausible, but they are not. Any doctrine that takes away from the deity of Christ and His completed work for our salvation is false and must be rejected. Paul is fearful that some may become deluded by these false teachers. He wants the believers to examine what they are being told. Is it true to what they have been taught and does it hold Jesus as the only way to salvation?

Paul's concern for the church at Colossae was well-founded. From the beginning of the church, there have been those who wanted to change the gospel by adding to it or taking from it. Many forms of false teachings have come to the church through the years. Today some accept a gospel that Jesus is not the Son of God. Some do not accept His resurrection as being a bodily resurrection. Many no longer believe the Bible to be the inerrant Word of God. How sad that many have become deluded by the false teachings of our day.

— Help me to encourage others to believe the Bible. —

> *For though I am absent in body, yet I am with*
> *you in spirit, rejoicing to see your good order and*
> *the firmness of your faith in Christ. (2:5)*

PAUL HAD never been to Colossae, but he wanted the believers to know that he was with them in spirit. He tells them that he rejoices with them because of their faith in Christ. Even though there were some false teachers who were troubling the church, the Christians were standing firm and holding on to the gospel. Paul was encouraging them to continue to stand firm. The early church, like the church today, faced many false teachings. Paul wants to ensure the believers that they are doing what is right by holding to the gospel that they have received. The Spirit of Christ binds together all who believe in Him. Paul wants the church to know of his support for them and the joy that they bring to him.

What a blessing it is that even when we are absent from other believers, we are joined with them in spirit. The Holy Spirit in all of us helps to unite our spirits in the bond of peace. So often we have to be separated from those we love — and having Christ in us and them gives us peace and assurance that God is with us, and all will be well. Regardless of the circumstances of life, we can have the peace of God that calms our hearts. Having other believers in fellowship with us, even though we are separated, is a real blessing. Paul's love and concern for the church at Colossae helped them to remain firm in their faith in Christ.

— Thank You, Lord, for the fellowship of other believers. —

Therefore, as you received Christ Jesus the Lord, so walk in him, rooted and built up in him and established in the faith, just as you were taught, abounding in thanksgiving. (2:6-7)

PAUL ENCOURAGES the Christians at Colossae to walk in the Lord. He says, "Since you have received Christ Jesus the Lord, then you are able to walk in Him." Paul is certain that they have been rooted in Christ and now wants them to be built up in their faith. Faith is established as we grow in it and learn the ways of the Lord. Paul states that these believers have been taught what was right and how to walk. He then says, "Abound in thanksgiving." Gratitude should be natural for a child of God. How often we forget to be grateful to God. As we walk with the Lord, He will give us many helps, for which we should be grateful. Paul wants to make sure that the believers do not forget that they owe a debt of thanksgiving to the Lord.

If we have received Christ Jesus the Lord, we are children of God. Being saved brings many blessings to each of us. It is necessary that we learn to be grateful for God's blessings. Being saved gives us the opportunity and responsibility of walking with the Lord. We must be sure that we are grounded in the faith and settled in Christ. Then we can grow in the grace and knowledge of Jesus. Our life in Christ should be a life of gratitude to God for all that He has done for us. Thanksgiving should result in "thanks living."

— Thank You, Jesus, for saving me for eternity. —

> *See to it that no one takes you captive by philosophy and empty deceit, according to human tradition, according to the elemental spirits of the world, and not according to Christ. (2:8)*

THIS VERSE gives us some insight into the problems that were in the church at Colossae. Dr. R.C. Sproul states: "It is notoriously difficult to reconstruct the false teach to which Paul responds in the book of Colossians because the letter is less a critique of error than a positive statement of the sufficiency of the person and work of Christ. The Colossians appear to have come under the influence of a combination of Jewish and pagan piety presenting itself as a philosophical system and insisting on submission to various astral or cosmic powers."

While we do not know the content of the false teachings, we can be sure that the teachings were causing the Colossians real problems. Any time that false doctrine comes into the church, there will always be those who are led astray by it. Paul warns against philosophy and empty deceit. Some of these teachers may have been presenting themselves as some kind of expert in understanding. Some of the teachings may have been parts of the Mosaic Law that would hinder a person's understanding of the sufficiency of the work of Christ. Today, many do not understand that salvation is by the grace of God alone through faith alone in Christ alone. Many traditions of men keep people from salvation in Christ.

— *May I be faithful to the true gospel.* —

> *For in him the whole fullness of deity dwells bodily, and you have been filled in him, who is the head of all rule and authority. (2:9-10)*

PAUL INSTRUCTS the believers that all they need is in Christ. He is the fullness of the Godhead and is the sufficient Savior of all who believe. God sent His Son to be the payment for our sin. The death, burial and resurrection of Jesus was the finished work that brought us salvation. The empty and vain philosophies of the world could not pay for sin. They have no standing with God. All rule and authority has been given to Jesus. In Christ we are complete. God did not ordain any other means for us to come to Him. The Son of God did the will of the Father by giving His life for our sin. Deity came among us and we beheld His glory, the glory of the only begotten Son of God.

In contrast to the false teachings, Paul states that Christ is all that we need. What Jesus accomplished in His life, death and resurrection is all that we need to bring us into relationship with God. Anyone who claims something needs to be added to the work of Christ is a false teacher. Jesus is sufficient for the work of redemption. He is Lord because He is Savior. God has given Him a Name above all names, that at the name of Jesus every knee shall bow, and every tongue confess that Jesus is Lord. All God requires is that we have faith in Jesus as our Savior and Lord. God has provided all He requires in His Son.

— *Jesus is the Supreme Savior and Lord of all who believe.* —

In him also you were circumcised with a circumcision made without hands, by putting off the body of the flesh, by the circumcision of Christ, having been buried with him in baptism, in which you were also raised with him through the powerful working of God, who raised him from the dead. (2:11-12)

PAUL MAY be mentioning circumcision here because some of the false teachers were like the Judaizers and said that circumcision was necessary to be a Christian. Paul also may have been showing that baptism was the sign of the new covenant just as circumcision had been the sign of the old covenant. Paul is not saying baptism is necessary for salvation, but that baptism is a picture of our surrender to Christ and our being buried with him and then raised to walk in new life. Christ has made it possible for us to come to God by faith alone.

Regardless of what the false teachers were telling the believers in Colossae, Paul wants them to know that all they need is faith in Jesus. While the Jews placed great importance on circumcision, it did not make a man a Jew. If he were born a Jew or became a Jew through teaching, he was to be circumcised in obedience to God. When a person accepts Jesus as Savior and Lord, he should be obedient in baptism. Baptism does not add anything to the work of Christ but is a symbol of our following the Lord. Paul wants all to know that salvation is in Christ alone through faith alone.

— We are saved by faith in the finished work of Jesus. —

And you, who were dead in your trespasses and the uncircumcision of your flesh, God made alive together with him, having forgiven us all our trespasses, by canceling the record of debt that stood against us with its legal demands. This he set aside, nailing it to the cross. (2:13-14)

PAUL RECOUNTS what these believers used to be. They were dead in trespasses and the uncircumcision of their flesh. They were not of the OT covenant people. Their sin had to be paid for before they could come to God. Jesus brought them to life when He paid for the sin debt they owed. The blood of Jesus cleanses us from all sin. Because Jesus was the sinless Son of God and a sinless man, He could make atonement for sin. Paul states that all the demands of the Law were taken out of the way and nailed to the cross in the person of Jesus Christ. John the Baptist had called Jesus "the lamb of God that takes away the sin of the world."

Paul wants to be clear that what man could not do in paying for sin, God did in the person of His Son. We were born with a sin nature, and we have no ability to change our nature. We are sinners by birth. We sin because we are sinners. The people at Colossae had to be born again if they were to come to salvation. God made that possible in Christ. The Spirit of God helps us come to know that we are lost and need a Savior. God allows us to come by faith to Him. It is all by the grace of God that brings us to Him.

— *Saved and kept by grace — praise the Lord.* —

> *He disarmed the rulers and authorities and put them to open shame, by triumphing over them in him. (2:15)*

PAUL TELLS us that Jesus conquered Satan and his demons when he died at Calvary. There was a battle between right and evil at the cross. Satan held people in bondage to the fear of death until Jesus conquered death. His victory opens the way for us to come into the presence of God. Paul says Jesus put the rulers and authorities to open shame. While it looked like Satan had won at Calvary, it was really his defeat. Death that had power over men had no power over the Son of man. He willingly submitted to death so that He could overcome its effects and release mankind from its grip.

His triumph was sure because He was the Son of God. He took the power of death and hell away from Satan and defeated him for eternity.

When Jesus died on Calvary, He was paying the sin debt we owed. Satan's power lies in his ability to tempt us to sin. Because we are born with a sin nature, sin becomes natural to us. Since Jesus was sinless, He could be tempted in all ways as we are, yet without sin. His death paid for sin for all who believe in Him. Satan's power was broken at the cross. Jesus defeated him then and will bring his ultimate defeat when He comes to set up His kingdom. We have been set free from the penalty of sin by the blood of Jesus. With the Spirit's help, we can overcome the power of sin in our lives. One day, we will be with Jesus and be free from the presence of sin.

— Praise God for the victory we have in Jesus. —

> *Therefore let no one pass judgment on you in questions of food and drink, or with regard to a festival or a new moon or a Sabbath. These are a shadow of things to come, but the substance belongs to Christ. (2:16-17)*

PAUL'S REFERENCE to food and drink, festivals, a new moon or a Sabbath may mean that some of the false teachers were trying to require that the believers in Colossae keep some of the requirements of the Old Covenant. The Law of Moses set out many regulations for the nation of Israel. Some Jews tried to bring those regulations over into the church. In Acts 15, there is a council that discusses the questions of what is required for a person to become a Christian. The council of apostles and elders decide that the keeping of practices of the Law are not necessary for salvation. Perhaps some at Colossae were being led to believe there were some regulations that they needed to follow.

Paul says that all a Christian needs is in Christ. He is now clear in telling them that the rules and regulations that some might want to bring over to the church from the Mosaic Law are not necessary. Paul states all of these things were only a shadow, but Christ is the substance (fulfillment) of all these requirements. If one is in Christ, then they are acceptable to God. Our acceptance does not depend upon us being able to keep certain rules. We come to Jesus by faith. The Law has been nailed to the cross, and Christ is our Savior.

— Thank You, Jesus, for being my all-sufficient Savior. —

> *Let no one disqualify you, insisting on asceticism and worship of angels, going on in detail about visions, puffed up without reason by his sensuous mind, and not holding fast to the Head, from whom the whole body, nourished and knit together through its joints and ligaments, grows with a growth that is from God. (2:18-19)*

ALTHOUGH WE don't know what the false teachings were at Colossae, we get some idea by Paul's rebuttal. He says to let no one disqualify you because you don't agree with them on their teachings. These teachings were requiring the believers to deny themselves (asceticism) and to worship angels. The teachers claimed they had visions, but Paul states they are puffed up in their sensuous minds. Their problem is they are not holding to the Head (Christ). The church can only be properly nurtured by the Head. In Him we are built up unto a holy church. Paul states the growth that the church needs comes from God. And it comes to the church through Christ.

The early church, like the church today, had many false teachers. Those who require anything but faith in the finished work of Jesus as a basis for salvation are false teachers. Today, many cults, and even some so-called churches, have many rules that one must follow to be a part of their group. The true church is made up of those who have been saved by the grace of God through faith in Jesus only.

— *May we be faithful to the Head of the church, Jesus.* —

If with Christ you died to the elemental spirits of the world, why, as if you were still alive in the world, do you submit to regulations — "Do not handle, Do not taste, Do not touch" (referring to things that all perish as they are used) — according to human precepts and teachings. (2:20-22)

PAUL NOW asks his readers, "If you died with Christ to the things of this world, why would you submit to the regulations regarding things that perish with their use?" We are to be in the world but not of the world. Possibly some of the false teachers were telling people they had to restrain from contact with the things in the world to be better Christians. Paul says all such teaching has to do with human precepts. It is what someone thinks, not what God requires. The things of this world are given to us by God to be used for His glory and our good. We are not to love things but are to use them properly.

Being in the world as a Christian is difficult. There is the constant temptation from the world to be like it. However, Paul says we are to be dead to the things of the world and alive unto Christ. When we have the right perspective of the world, we can walk with God and be a help to others. Those who want us to withdraw from the world are asking us to not be the light and salt that God wants us to be. As Dr. David Jeremiah says, "Being a Christian is not hard; it is impossible."

Only by the grace of God can we be the person God wants us to be in this world.

— May I walk as a child of light in this dark world. —

> *These have indeed an appearance of wisdom in promoting self-made religion and asceticism and severity to the body, but they are of no value in stopping the indulgence of the flesh. (2:23)*

PAUL STATES that these regulations have the appearance of wisdom in promoting self-made religion and asceticism and severity to the body. Maybe some of the false teachers were leading people in practices that were harmful and hurtful to the body. Those who were willing to submit to the practices suggested by false teachers may have thought the regulations helped them in their Christian growth. Paul is warning such practices are of no value in stopping the indulgence of the flesh. We all like ourselves more than we are willing to admit. Perhaps the false teachers were suggesting practices that were supposed to help control the flesh, but Paul says that is not going to help.

To indulge the flesh is to give in to its desires. There is a constant battle not to give in to the flesh. Perhaps the false teachers were saying, "Here is what you do." Paul says all the regulations are of no use in controlling the flesh. As Christians, we must surrender our bodies to the Lord. When we seek to walk faithfully with Jesus, He will help us get our flesh under control. Because we are still in the flesh after we are saved, we will have to battle with the flesh. We are warned many times in the Bible about our battles with Satan, the world and the flesh. In Jesus, we can have victory.

— *Help me to love You, Lord, and be faithful in my walk.* —

CHAPTER THREE

If then you have been raised with Christ, seek the things that are above, where Christ is seated, at the right hand of God. (3:1)

PAUL HAS been warning about the dangers of the false teachings. Now he points the believers to the realities of being saved. "If' can also be translated "since." It is a truth that those who have been saved have been raised with Christ. We were dead in trespasses and sin, but God quickened us to life. We are now a part of God's heavenly kingdom. Paul tells us to seek the things that are above. In Ephesians, Paul tells us we are seated in heavenly places in Christ. Here he says Christ is seated at the right hand of God and we are seated in Him. Heaven is reality for the believer. We need to focus our attention more on how we can please God.

It is a wonderful blessing to be "in Christ." When we are born again, we are placed in Christ. Christ is now in heaven seated at the right hand of God. Therefore, we are in Christ in heavenly places. Too often we allow the things of this world to keep us from enjoying our position in Christ. Of course, we can go too far to the other extreme. There is an old saying that states: "Some people are so heavenly minded that they are no earthly good." Christian maturity has the goal of living in this world in such a way that God is honored and glorified by our lives.

— Help me to keep balance between earth and heaven. —

Set your minds on things that are above, not on things that are on earth. (3:2)

AS CHRISTIANS, Paul wants the believers to learn to think properly. There is a battle that goes on in the mind of every believer. We must learn to think about this world in the way that God would have us think. The natural man thinks only in the ways of the world. The saved man must learn to think in supernatural ways. "Set our minds on things above" does not mean that we forget about our earthly existence, but it means we begin to see how God is leading us in our lives. Considering what God wants done in us is a part of growing in the grace and knowledge of Christ. The things of earth that used to control our thoughts are to be put aside as we seek the things above. It is a blessing to be part of God's family, but it requires us to learn to walk as God's children.

Paul urges all believers to begin to focus our minds on the things of God. A popular hymn says: "Turn your eyes upon Jesus, look full in His wonderful face, and the things of earth will grow strangely dim, in the light of His glory and grace." Setting our minds on things above is a constant battle. The devil wants to bring doubts and questions into our minds. He will seek to turn our minds away from God by any means he can. That is why we must set (make a decision) to put our minds on things above so we can grow in Christ. The things of earth can draw us away from God, and we must be aware of that fact.

— Lord, I want my mind set on You. —

*For you have died, and your life is hidden
with Christ in God. (3:3)*

PAUL IS stating here one of the great truths of the gospel. Christ not only died for us, but we died in Him. Jesus took our sin and paid for it in full. His death, burial and resurrection make it possible for us to be reconciled to God. Because Jesus died our death, we are included in that death. Paul is making it plain that we died to sin when we were born again by the Spirit through faith in Jesus. Our sin was paid for at Calvary, and we receive that forgiveness in the new birth. God places us in Christ, and we are kept by God for all eternity. To be hidden in Christ means that our life can never be lost to God because we are secure in Christ. Since we have been saved by faith in Jesus, we are secure by Jesus forever.

Hidden with Christ is a mystery of the work of God at our salvation. We may not understand all that happened when we got saved. But we can be sure that our salvation is eternal. Jesus gives us everlasting life, and we shall never perish. When I think about being hidden in Christ, I think about the fact that the devil can't get to me. No matter how much the devil wants to have me, he can't. My life is no longer my own; I have been brought with a price — the precious blood of Jesus. Hidden and secure I am in Christ and will be for all eternity. Praise be to God, who has given us life in His Son.

— Thank You, Father, I am hidden in Christ. —

> *When Christ who is your life appears, then you
> also will appear with him in glory. (3:4)*

PAUL WANTS his readers (and us) to focus their minds on the return of Christ. All he is asking them to do is important, because one day they will be with Jesus. Paul states: "When Christ who is your life appears." Paul has taught them about the return of Christ, and now he is helping them to understand how important remembering that truth is. When Christ appears, we will appear with Him in glory. That is a statement of fact. We can believe it and know that it is true because God promised it. As Jesus was ascending into heaven, God sent two angels to tell the disciples that this same Jesus would come again. Paul is saying we have the assurance that when Christ does come, we will be with Him. God keeps His promises, and we can be sure of that.

The return of Christ is the next event on God's calendar. We cannot know the day or the hour, but we can know that Jesus is coming. Paul gives us some insight into that event in 1 Thessalonians 4:13-17. Then in verse 18, he says: "Encourage one another with these words." What an encouragement it is to know that one day we will see Jesus. He may come in our lifetime, but if He does not, we will see Him when He calls us home. The song writer said: "O, that will be glory for me." What a day of rejoicing it will be, to be with Jesus in glory. He will come for the church (or each of us) to be with Him forever.

— *I am looking for Your coming, Jesus.* —

Put to death therefore what is earthly in you: sexual immorality, impurity, passion, evil desire, and covetousness, which is idolatry. On account of these the wrath of God is coming. (3:5-6)

PAUL NOW encourages the believers to become in practice what they are in principle — dead to sin. The action of putting to death signifies their need to put into practice the holy traits that God has placed in them. They are now the children of God, and Paul says they should live like the children of God. Some of the false teachers may have been telling the believers there were certain physical practices they need to become better Christians. Paul is saying that putting these evil desires to death will help them as they set their minds on things above. Simply trying to clean up one's life is not the point. The point is to learn to be more like Jesus. Four of the five things he lists are sexual in nature. The fifth — covetousness — Paul says is the same as idolatry.

Paul warns the believers that the wrath of God comes on those who live by such practices. Colossae was filled with pagan worship, much of which involved sexual acts. Men and women were prostitutes in the pagan temples. Sex was viewed as being a part of the worship of the false gods. Paul now tells these new Christians they must put away these practices. All the sexual perversion of Colossae had to be put away from them. He also warns them that covetousness is idolatry and must be put away.

— Help me to put away evil desires. —

In these you too once walked, when you were living in them. (3:7)

PAUL REMINDS the believers of their lifestyles before they came to the gospel and were saved. Maybe some of them had fallen back into some of their old habits. Maybe some of them were being judgmental of those who were still living a pagan lifestyle. Paul says, "You too once walked in these evil ways." God saves us because we need to be saved. Not all of the new believers had been doing all these evil things, but they all had sin that needed to be forgiven. We are born with a nature that is contrary to God. We know how to do evil things because of our evil nature. Not all of us are as bad as we could be but, all of us are sinners. Turning from that sinful life is part of our growth in Christ. Paul wants the believers and us to remember where God brought us from so that we are not drawn back into those old habits.

One of the wonderful facts about salvation is that God makes us new creations in Jesus. Old things pass away, and we are new. Our old nature is changed into a new creation. As Christians, it is easy to forget how bad we were — and some may not have been really bad. It is not what we *do* that condemns us, it is what we *are*. We are sinners in need of a Savior. We are separated from God by our sin and cannot come to God in any way except through faith in Jesus. Paul warns us to remember what we were and to help others come out of that sin into salvation in Jesus.

— I am thankful I am not what I used to be. —

But now you must put them all away: anger, wrath, malice, slander, and obscene talk from your mouth. (3:8)

PAUL CONTINUES to list those traits that must be changed in the life of the believers. He makes it a must-do for them. They must put away anger. Anger is one of the problems that many battle. Anger is caused when we think someone has done something against us or to us. The Bible warns, "Don't let the sun go down on your anger." Anger is not always wrong because we can be angry at sin. What I try to do is say that I need to be angry at anything that hurts Jesus, but not at things that might upset me. Put away wrath and malice; these two go hand in hand. We display wrath when we strike out at others. Malice is thinking we are justified to display our wrath. Slander is speaking lies about others and saying it is the truth. Avoiding gossip is the best policy. Obscene talk fills our world, and if we are not careful it can become a habit for us. Watching what we say and how we say it is the best habit.

When we were lost, the things listed by Paul didn't bother us. Now Paul says we must change our attitude toward these evil actions. It is easy to think we can do some of these things and be right with God. Paul warns us our fellowship with God demands that we put away these evil practices. As Christians, we are to represent Jesus to the lost world. We cannot do that if we act like they act. Our witness to the lost demands that we live close to God and show them Jesus in us reaching to them in love.

— Help me, Lord, to avoid the evil ways of the world. —

> *Do not lie to one another, seeing that you have put off the old self with its practices and have put on the new self, which is being renewed in knowledge after the image of its creator. (3:9-10)*

PAUL TELLS the believers, "Do not lie to one another." Most of the time when we lie to others, we have already lied to ourselves. Paul says that is the action of the old nature. You have put off the old self and its practices. He has just told them they must do this. The old self is gone, and the new self has been put on. The old gospel song says: "The best thing I ever did do was take off the old coat and put on the new." Paul represents salvation as a change of garments. We were once children of darkness, but we are now children of light. God changed us by His grace. When we came by faith to Jesus, He saved us and put us into the kingdom of light.

Paul encourages the believers by telling them that the new self is being renewed in knowledge after the image of its creator, God. We have a know-so salvation. God has given to us eternal life and that life is in His Son. We can know we are saved because the Spirit of God bears witness to our spirit that we are the children of God. Many fail to accept eternal security, but that is what God has promised and given to all who believe on the Lord Jesus Christ. Our knowledge comes from the Word of God that is taught to us by the Spirit of God.

Jesus told His disciples that the Spirit of truth would lead them into all truth. That promise is for us also.

— *Praise God, I am a new creation in Christ.* —

Here there is not Greek and Jew, circumcised or uncircumcised, barbarian, Scythian, slave, free; but Christ is all, and in all. (3:11)

PAUL IS showing that the believers are all one in Christ. All of the cultural differences that seem to separate them are no longer true. There is no distinction between the believers. While they are indeed different, those differences are no longer important. In Christ, there is a unity that the world knows nothing about. This was a real problem for the early church just as it is a problem today. Some in the church believed they were better than others because of their background. The Jews thought of themselves as the only people of God. The Greeks considered everyone who was not a Greek as barbarians. Paul tells them that in Christ we are all included and all on an equal footing.

The early church had to battle the culture that divided people into different groups. That is still a real problem today. But Paul breaks down all those barriers when he states that Christ is all and in all. Jesus is no respecter of persons, and neither should we be. God sent His Son into the world that men might be saved. All nations are included in God's plan of salvation. Jesus told us to go into all the world with the gospel. We must not allow our prejudices to keep us from sharing the gospel with all those we know. The Cross is the great equalizer — all may come and be saved. Paul wanted us to understand that fact and share it with others.

— May I help send the gospel to the whole world. —

> *Put on then, as God's chosen ones, holy and beloved,*
> *compassionate hearts, kindness, humility, meekness,*
> *and patience, bearing with one another, and if one has a*
> *complaint against another, forgiving each other, as the Lord*
> *has forgiven you, so you must also forgive. (3:12-13)*

AS PAUL is telling the believers how to walk with the Lord, he continues to tell them what characteristics they must have. He says that since you are God's chosen, you are to be holy. Put on compassionate hearts, kindness, meekness and patience. These are the fruit of the Spirit in us. We are to walk in the Spirit and not fulfill the lusts of the flesh. When we have these fruit in us, we can then bear with one another. We must always be willing to forgive others just as the Lord has forgiven us. Only by being led by the Spirit are we able to do what God wants us to do.

The believers in Colossae were living in a wicked culture, just as we are. Paul wanted them to live holy lives so they could be a witness to those around them. This is the responsibility of every Christian. As we are going along in life, we are to be witnesses for the grace of God. If we will follow the Spirit and walk in the Spirit, we can be the people of God. God has given us His Spirit and His Word to help us walk with Him. The world will always be contrary to God and His people. We can help those in darkness to see the light by letting the light of Jesus shine through us.

— Father, thank You for allowing me to walk with You. —

And above all these put on love, which binds everything together in perfect harmony. (3:14)

PAUL HAS been encouraging the believers to seek to have the characteristics of Christ. The Spirit is given to us so that we can have the fruit of the Spirit to help us walk with God. After all the traits that Paul has listed, he now says above all of these put on love. Love is the characteristic that binds all the believer's walk to make it pleasing to God. God is love, and He desires that His children seek that love and show that love to others. Jesus told His disciples, "The world will know you are My disciples if you have love one for another." Paul is assuring the Christians at Colossae that exhibiting the love of Jesus will bring them into harmony with God and with each other. We are to be people who love God and others.

The Christian life is hard for anyone to follow. But God provides all that we need. By giving us His Word to teach us and His Spirit to guide us, we have all that is necessary for us to be able to walk with God. As we allow the Spirit to live the life of Christ in us, we will begin to show the fruit of the Spirit and our character will be changed. God is able to will and to do His good pleasure in us and through us. If we will seek to love others the way that God loves us, we will be able to be pleasing to the Father. The love of God is so amazing that we can never fully understand it, but we can learn from it how to love others. God loves us unconditionally; we should seek to love others the same.

— *Thank You, Lord, for Your amazing love.* —

And let the peace of Christ rule in your hearts, to which indeed you were called in one body. And be thankful. (3:15)

THERE IS no peace in a person's life that will last if it is not the peace of Christ. The world may want peace, but real peace only comes from God. Paul is telling the believers that if they will let the peace of God rule in their lives, they will find real unity in the church and will be a light to those around them. Colossae was a pagan city, and the believers there were under constant pressure to turn back to their sinful ways. Paul says the church is the body of Christ, into which you have been called. Christ can, and will, give you His peace. Jesus told His disciples: "My peace I give unto you, not as the world gives." The peace of Christ is beyond our understanding, but it is not beyond our acceptance.

Letting the peace of Christ rule in our hearts is easier said than done. The world wants us to be in turmoil. The devil is pleased when we are upset and worried. Often we try to hide our worry by saying, "I am just concerned." It is easy for concern to turn to worry. But if we will think about all that God does for us, we can stay focused on the peace that Christ gives us. We have been brought from darkness to the light of the gospel. We have been saved from our sin for eternity. There really is not anything in this world that can cause us to lose our salvation. When I think of all God's blessings, then I am thankful. Paul says the peace of God makes us thankful.

— *God's peace makes me thankful for His blessings.* —

*Let the word of Christ dwell in you richly, teaching
and admonishing one another in all wisdom,
singing psalms and hymns and spiritual songs, with
thankfulness in your hearts to God. (3:16)*

PAUL INVITES the believers to share with each other the word of Christ and His wisdom. The word of Christ gives us the information we need to serve God and others. The wisdom of God enables us to properly apply God's Word to our lives. When we have the word of Christ in us, then we can seek the wisdom of God to help us be of use to others. Paul tells the church to teach and admonish one another in all wisdom. He encourages them to sing psalms, hymns and spiritual songs to lift them up and to fill them with thankfulness. We learn to be grateful by remembering all that the Lord has done for us and all that He has promised to us. A heart filled with the Word of Christ will also be filled with gratitude to God.

One real problem in the church today is spiritual ignorance. Many Christians do not know the Word of God. Some have even rejected the truth that God's Word is infallible. God has given us His Word and protected it so that we can know it can be trusted. Paul tells the church at Colossae to let the Word of Christ dwell richly in them. When we have the Word of God in us, we are better able to walk in obedience to God. Hiding God's Word in our hearts will help us to avoid the sins that so easily beset us.

— May I love Your Word, Lord. —

*And whatever you do, in word or deed, do everything
in the name of the Lord Jesus, giving thanks to
God the Father through Him. (3:17)*

PAUL SUMS up his point by encouraging the believers to do all that they do, in word or deed, in the name of the Lord Jesus, and to give thanks to God the Father through Jesus. Our words and actions should agree. We say, "Don't talk the talk if you can't walk the walk." But in truth, we are often hypocrites. We do not set out to say one thing and do another, but it happens. If we will fill our hearts with the Word of Christ and let the Spirit live the life of Christ in us, we can begin to overcome this sin. Whatever we do should be done to bring glory to God. Jesus tells us that we are to do our good works so men will see them and give glory to the Father. Our good works should help others know that God is real in us and is doing His work in and through us.

If we would strive to live a life of thanksgiving to God, it would help us not to sin against Him with our words and deeds. Gratitude helps us remember and appreciate all the blessings that God gives to us and all the promises He has fulfilled to us and in us. I cannot live the Christian life. I must be willing to surrender to the Spirit of God in me. As Paul says in Galatians, "The life I now live I live by the life of the Son of God in me." God gives us His Spirit so that we can become more like Jesus, His Son. We should be grateful for God's gifts and the Spirit's guidance.

— *May all I do and say please You, Lord.* —

Wives, submit to your husbands, as is fitting in the Lord. (3:18)

PAUL NOW begins instructions for the family. He first addresses the wives. Wives in Paul's day were viewed as possessions of their husbands. Christianity brought about a whole new way of looking at the family and wives in particular. The Jewish believers had grown up thinking women were inferior to men. The Greek world did little to show respect or care of women. So as Paul addresses the families of his day, he starts by saying that the wives are to submit to their husbands. This would have been the situation in most homes of that day. But Paul adds, "As is fitting in the Lord." Wives are to submit to their husbands because they are in submission to the Lord. As a Christian, the wife has placed herself in submission to the Lord. To show that submission, she places herself in submission to her husband.

Probably no other part of the Christian home is under attack more than the idea of wives submitting to their husbands. Part of this is because of the misunderstanding that men think they are more important than women. While that might be true in some religions, it is not true in Christianity. In Christ, we are all equal. But God has established the family with certain guidelines. Wives are to submit to their husbands. But first, and most important, both husband and wife are to submit to the Lord. When that takes place, then wives can submit to their husbands because it is fitting in the Lord.

— Help me to be the husband my wife needs me to be. —

Husbands, love your wives, and do not be harsh with them. (3:19)

HAVING ADDRESSED the wife, Paul now turns to the husband. He states that the husband is to love his wife and not be harsh to her. In Paul's day, husbands treated their wives in any manner they wished. Many husbands kept concubines as well as their wives. Christ brought back the truth of the law: Marriage is for one man with one woman. Now Paul is striving to help these husbands know how to live with their wives. If a husband loves his wife as he should, the wife will not have a problem being in submission to the husband. Too often, husbands want wives to submit to them when they are not being the leader and provider God told them to be. It is the man's responsibility to provide, protect and lead the home. He is to allow his wife to be his helpmate as he leads.

Many men are unwilling to submit to the Lord as they should. Therefore, they cannot love their wives as they should, and the wives will have a hard time being in submission. When Paul states, "Do not be harsh with your wife," he is telling the husbands that they are to be kind and gentle with their wife. If a man loves the Lord as God asks him to, he will be able to love his wife as he should. Too often, men love themselves more than they love their wives. As a Christian, I am to love God first and my wife as myself. This will allow me to be pleasing to God and a help to my wife. When I show the love of God to my wife, she can submit to me without fear.

— *Help me to love my wife the way You love me.* —

Children, obey your parents in everything,
for this pleases the Lord. (3:20)

PAUL TURNS now to the children. He is writing to Christian parents. He wants their children to learn to be obedient to them. There are many parents who are not Christian but are also not good parents. But if a child has Christian parents, then he or she is to obey them in everything. This puts a great responsibility on the parents. They are to train their children and teach them the ways of the Lord. God gives us clear instructions in the Bible on what we are to teach our children and how we are to guide them. Children must be taught truth and must be guided to come to the Lord for salvation. Too often, parents neglect to teach their children the gospel. The church can, and should, help parents — but the parents should be the first to teach their children about the things of God.

Children by nature are sinners. We sometimes forget that fact. As I heard one preacher say, "You parents need to remember you are raising the devil's kids." Each child needs to learn to obey their parents so they can one day come to obey the call of God on their life. Sin separates us from God, and until we come to understand that we will never be willing to come to God for salvation. Parents are to live Jesus before their children so that those children can see that they need Jesus. Teaching our children about Jesus will help them be able to obey us and Him.

— Lord, help parents to teach their children to obey. —

*Fathers, do not provoke your children, lest
they become discouraged. (3:21)*

BOTH PARENTS are to teach their children to obey. Paul now addresses the fathers about this matter. He tells the fathers do not provoke your children. This is a real problem for some of us men. We get upset and say or do things we should not do, to our children or around our children. Sometimes the way we treat their mother causes our children to want to stay clear of us. Sometimes our harsh words, even though unintended, hurt our children. Being a father requires that we be in submission to Jesus. The Spirit of God in us will not help us if we will not submit to Him. Then and only then can we learn how to teach our children. My actions and words must be led by God's Spirit so that I do not provoke my children. I want them to listen to me and learn from me how to walk with Jesus.

Being a Christian father gives me the opportunity to show my children what God has done for me and what He is willing to do for them. If I am not being obedient to the Lord, I have no right to demand my children be obedient to me. I never have the right to demand their obedience, but I should get their obedience by showing them the love of God. For some men it is difficult to learn how to encourage their children. Paul warns us if we provoke them, they can become discouraged. May we seek to encourage and uplift our children as we help them come to Jesus.

— Fathers, seek God's help in leading your children. —

Bond-servants, obey in everything those who are your earthly masters, not by way of eye service, as people-pleasers, but with sincerity of heart, fearing the Lord. (3:22)

PAUL NOW turns to the slaves who were in the church. Slavery was a part of the culture of that day, and many slaves had come to faith in Jesus. Paul wants them to know they are to obey their earthly masters — not with eye service as people-pleasers but with sincerity of heart, fearing the Lord. Paul wants them to understand they are to be obedient because they belong to the Lord. Their testimony should not be harmed by the way they do their work. We have all known people who only worked when the boss was watching. That what Paul is addressing. Some slaves were treated horribly, but others were treated kindly. Whatever the situation, the bond-servants were to obey their earthly masters.

Since we have not lived in slavery, it is hard to imagine how difficult it could be. But Paul's concern is that the slaves be the best workers they could be so that their masters might be influenced for Christ. Often, Christians forget that they are to be good employees so that they might be a witness to those around them. Doing the best we can do should always be a part of being a Christian witness. Paul tells the bond-servants to remember they are to fear the Lord. If we would always remember that we are to be pleasing to the Lord, we would be better workers. Sometimes being a Christian helps us to be a better worker.

— *May my work be pleasing to You, Lord.* —

Whatever you do, work heartily, as for the Lord and not for men, knowing that from the Lord you will receive the inheritance as your reward. You are serving the Lord Christ. (3:23-24)

PAUL SUMS up his remarks on working by stating, "Whatever you do, work heartily, as for the Lord." As believers, they were to know that what they did was to help their witness. If they were good workers and people took notice, they could tell others, "I am a Christian, and I do my work to please the Lord." Paul tells them they are serving the Lord and they will receive their reward. While it is true that they were being paid for their work, that should not be the reason for them doing a good job. God does reward us with physical things at times, but our eternal reward is in heaven with Him. We may be materially blessed by God for the work we do, but that is only a small taste of the reward to come.

As Christians, we are to be servants of the Lord. Paul reminds the believers and us that the work we do we should do the best we can. We are not only working for an earthly boss, but we have a heavenly master that we want to please. Too many Christians fail to see that the work God has given them is a blessing. That is especially true if we are working with people who may not like us or want to help us. We will have tribulations in this world. But God assures us of an eternal reward when we seek to serve Him and be a help to others.

— My work will be rewarded far more than I deserve. —

*For the wrongdoer will be paid back for the wrong
he has done, and there is no partiality. (3:25)*

DOING A good job brings rewards. Paul says those who do wrong will also receive a payment. Wrongdoers will be paid back for the wrong they have done. God does not show favorites. When we do good, we receive a reward for our good work. When we do evil, we receive the consequences of that evil. Maybe some in the church at Colossae were not doing what they could to provide for themselves or to help others. As Dr. Bob Jones Sr. used to say, "It is never wrong to do right, and it is never right to do wrong." Those who live wicked lives will have to answer for their evil doings. We need to warn those who reject the gospel that there are consequences they will not like.

As Christians, we are to do what is right according to God. We cannot be caught up in the evil of this world and act like it does not matter. Paul is warning the believers at Colossae and us that we are to turn away from evil every time we can. Some do wrong without any thought of the trouble it might bring to them or others. God is willing to forgive our sins when we confess them. But God will not forgive unconfessed sins. He is fair to all by providing Jesus as our Savior. Those who reject Jesus will be punished for their sin.

There is not an opportunity for sin to be overlooked by God. He sees all our sin, He forgives when we ask to be forgiven, and He judges and condemns when we reject His forgiveness.

— Help me to warn wrongdoers about their future. —

CHAPTER FOUR

*Masters, treat your bondservants
justly and fairly, knowing that you
also have a Master in heaven. (4:1)*

PAUL GIVES the masters of slaves a clear instruction. They are to treat their slaves justly and fairly. They are to remember that they have a Master in heaven. Those who were Christians and owned slaves had a special requirement on them. They were to be good to their slaves. This was a part of their witness to the slaves and to others. The Bible does not approve of slavery but addresses the situation of the first century world. Many were slaves, and some were treated badly. Paul wants the Christian masters to set a different standard for their slaves. Because they would have to answer to God, these Christian slave owners were held to a higher standard than those in the world.

While we may not know much about slavery as an institution, we know about being slaves to sin. I cannot imagine how hard it would have been to be a slave to another person. So Paul warns these slave holders to be careful in the way they treat their slaves. Masters and slaves had both come to Christ. Now a new relationship existed, for the master and the slave were now brothers in Christ. Neither the master nor the slave was to take advantage of his new situation. Slaves were still to obey their masters, and masters were to treat their slaves fairly. This was a new concept for both of them.

— *May I treat others justly and fairly.* —

Continue steadfastly in prayer, being watchful in it with thanksgiving. (4:2)

PAUL HAS already thanked the church for their prayers and support. Now he asks them to continue steadfastly in prayer. Paul knew that one of the best actions the believers could take was to pray. We can do more *after* we pray, but we need to do nothing *until* we have prayed. Paul knew that many prayers were the reason God had guided him and his companions. He encourages the church to be watchful in prayer with thanksgiving. Sometimes we pray — and when God answers our prayers, we forget to thank Him. Thanksgiving should always be a part of our prayers. Paul wants these new believers to know that prayer is a vital part of growing in Christ. We can call on the God of the universe and He will hear us. God hears and answers prayer. James says we have not because we ask not. We sometimes ask amiss, and God does not answer our selfish prayers.

The missionary journeys of Paul are filled with times that he asked prayer for himself and the work he was doing. God is pleased when we call upon Him. God has made it possible for us to pray to Him so that we can know He hears and answers us. God always answers our prayers. He says yes, no, or wait. Our problem is that often we pray and try to tell God how to answer. He is sovereign; we are not. He knows what is best and always works for our good and His glory. We can trust Him, for He knows what is best.

— Thank You, Lord, for the privilege of prayer. —

At the same time, pray also for us, that God may open a door for the word, to declare the mystery of Christ, on account of which I am in prison — that I may make it clear, which is how I ought to speak. (4:3-4)

PAUL ASKED the church to pray for him and his work. He wants them to ask God to open a door for the preaching of the gospel. The mystery of Christ is the good news that Jesus died for our sins, was buried, and on the third day rose again. The gospel that Paul preached was to some foolishness, but to those who believed it was life and blessing. Paul states, "I am in prison because of preaching the gospel." But he says, "I don't want to quit or change the message." Paul wanted to be clear with the message and wanted the believers to pray that he would remain faithful. He knew that the prayers of the church at Colossae were a part of the blessings that God had given to him in his labors.

Paul was aware that he needed the prayers of others. He was indeed a prayer warrior, but he wanted others to pray with him and for him. One of the great blessings we have is to pray for others. How sad that sometimes we tell people we will pray for them and then forget to do it. Having a prayer list helps us to keep others in mind when we go to prayer. God wants us to talk to Him about any and everything. He wants to hear from us about our needs, and then He wants us to hold others up to Him. The gospel song says: "Prayer is the key to heaven, but faith unlocks the door." James said that when we pray, we are to believe God hears and will act on our behalf. God always answers in the way that is best for us and those we pray for. Praise the Lord, He hears and answers our prayers.

— May I pray for others as You lead me. —

*Walk in wisdom toward outsiders, making
the best use of the time. (4:5)*

TIME IS a precious gift from God. We each have the same amount of it each day. How we use our time is of great concern to God. Paul tells the church at Colossae to walk in wisdom toward outsiders. Those who are not believers need to have us who are saved to be wise in how we deal with them. Wisdom is a gift from God, and James tells us if we lack wisdom we can ask God to give it to us. It is becoming more and more difficult in our day to walk in wisdom in this world. It was also difficult for the believers in Colossae. Paul encourages them to make good use of the time they have to influence those outside the faith. The early church was misunderstood in many of the cities where they had been founded. It took wisdom to help outsiders come to know what the gospel was about. Many false stories about the early church had to be dealt with, and that took wisdom.

While Paul is urging the believers at Colossae to use their time wisely, he is also telling us to do so. We need the wisdom of God to walk in our world. Far too many people today have little or no use for God. We live in an age that has turned away from God. As Christians, we need the wisdom of God as we deal with those who are lost. We need to remember what we were like before we were saved. We were strangers and aliens to the things of God. But by God's grace, someone told us about Jesus and the Spirit helped us to know we need Jesus. That is the opportunity we have today. In our dark world, the light of the gospel can shine brightly as we share Jesus with others. May we wisely use the time God gives us to take the gospel to others. Those who are lost need to come to Jesus before it is too late.

— Help me to be a good witness for You, Jesus. —

Let your speech always be gracious, seasoned with salt, so that you may know how you ought to answer each person. (4:6)

JAMES WARNS us that the tongue is a world of iniquity. That is not to be the case for a Christian. Paul encourages the believers (and us) to let our speech be gracious. He says, "Let your speech be seasoned with salt." Salt was used to preserve meats and other food in ancient days. In that way, meats and some other foods could be used for a longer period of time. Jesus told His disciples, "You are the salt of the earth." Jesus and Paul were both pointing to the helpful influence Christians can be. It is easy at times to say the wrong thing, sometimes without even meaning to or thinking about it. James warns that the tongue can set a world on fire. We cannot tame our tongue, but the Spirit can. Paul wants believers to put themselves under the control of the Spirit and then their speech can be gracious.

What we say and how we say it are always important as we deal with the world in which we live. Too often, we may say the right thing but in a wrong manner. Dr. Jack Hyles used to say, "I never apologize for my position (what I believe) but I have had to apologize many times for my disposition (how I said what I said)." Seasoning our speech with salt requires that we listen to the Spirit in us and allow Him to control our tongues and thoughts. I do not always know what to say, but if I will take the time to ask the Spirit for help, He will help me. We must take the time to think about what to say when we deal with the lost. They will not be helped by our being judgmental or critical. God can help us know how to speak to those who need Him. May we seek to listen to and obey the Spirit in our speech.

— May I be a good witness in my speech. —

> *Tychicus will tell you all about my activities. He is a beloved brother and faithful minister and fellow servant in the Lord. I have sent him to you for this very purpose, that you may know how we are and that he may encourage your hearts, and with him Onesimus, our faithful and beloved brother, who is one of you. They will tell you of everything that has taken place. (4:7-9)*

AS PAUL closes his letter, he gives some personal greetings to the church. He says, "I have sent Tychicus to you to tell you how I am doing and what has been going on." Paul says Tychicus was a beloved brother and faithful minister. He is the one who brought the letter from Paul to the church. Also, Paul says, "I have sent Onesimus, a faithful and beloved brother." Onesimus is the slave who ran away from Philemon. Paul had met him and led him to the Lord. He also was with Tychicus and was to report on the events that they had seen. He also was instructed by Paul to return to his master, and Paul sent a letter with him to Philemon. Paul wants the church at Colossae to know how he is doing and how the work is going in Rome.

It is good to have those who labor with us in the work of the Lord. Paul was glad to have these men help him. He trusted them and gave them the letter he had written to the church. He wanted the church to receive these men and hear them as they reported on the work at Rome. Even though Paul was in prison, he still had the opportunity to tell others about Christ. He says in the letter to the Romans that all the Roman guards have heard the gospel. A guard was chained to Paul, and Paul took that opportunity to share Jesus with the guard. We should be thankful for those who help us in our work for the Lord.

— *Father, I thank You for faithful workers in the kingdom.* —

Aristarchus my fellow prisoner greets you, and Mark the cousin of Barnabas (concerning whom you have received instructions — if he comes to you, welcome him), and Jesus who is called Justus. These are the only men of the circumcision among my fellow workers for the kingdom of God, and they have been a comfort to me. (4:10-11)

PAUL SENDS greetings from Aristarchus, whom he calls his fellow prisoner. Aristarchus was a Macedonian of Thessalonica who traveled with Paul on his third missionary journey. When Paul was put in prison in Rome, Aristarchus came to Rome and ministered to Paul in prison. Paul also says Mark is with him. This is John Mark, who had been with Paul and Barnabas on the first missionary journey but had turned back before the mission was completed. Later, Paul and Barnabas had disagreement about John Mark and separated, with Barnabas taking John Mark and Paul taking Silas as his new companion. However, in writing to the Romans, Paul had asked that Mark be brought to him. Paul instructs the church that if Mark comes to them, they are to welcome him. Paul also says that Jesus, who is called Justus, is with him.

Paul states that these are the only men of the circumcision who are with him. These Jewish men had come to believe the gospel and were now workers with Paul in the ministry. Paul states that "they have been a comfort to me." Paul was a strong man, but even he needed the help of others. He was glad that these men and others were with him during his time in Rome. Paul was not upset that he was in prison because he knew that he was doing the will of God. He was grateful that God had sent others to help him. Paul wanted the church to know about these helpers so they could pray for them also.

— *Thank You, Lord, for those who have helped me in Your work.* —

> *Epaphras, who is one of you, a servant of Christ Jesus, greets you, always struggling on your behalf in his prayers, that you may stand mature and fully assured in all the will of God. For I bear him witness that he has worked hard for you and for those in Laodicea and in Hierapolis. (4:12-13)*

PAUL NOW mentions Epaphras, who is from Colossae. He was probably the founder of the church in Colossae. Scholars believe that he was converted under Paul's ministry at Ephesus and went back home to preach the gospel. Paul acknowledges that Epaphras was from Colossae. Epaphras had gone to Rome to talk to Paul about the church. Paul's letter was in response to the visit of Epaphras. He stayed with Paul and continued to pray for the church at Colossae. Paul states that Epaphras worked hard for the believers at Colossae and also for those in Laodicea and Hierapolis. These were three cities that formed a sort of triangle. Most scholars believe that Paul instructed the church at Colossae to share his letter with the other two churches. The church at Laodicea was one of the churches that the apostle John addressed in the Revelation.

While not a great deal is known about Epaphras, Paul considered him a great servant of Jesus Christ. He was probably saved under Paul's preaching in Ephesus. He was from Colossae and is believed to have started the church there. He had gone to Rome to see Paul and tell him about the situation in Colossae. We do not know exactly what the false teachers were teaching at Colossae, but it concerned Epaphras enough to seek Paul's help. Today, we need more men like Epaphras who will stand up for the truth and will pray that others will come to know the truth of the gospel and share it with those around them. We are to be His witnesses wherever we are placed.

— God, give us faithful servants for the kingdom of Christ. —

Luke the beloved physician greets you, as does Demas. (4:14)

LUKE WAS the traveling companion of Paul and author of the gospel of Luke and the book of Acts. He was called a physician but may not have been of the wealthy class of that day. Dr. R.C. Sproul says that some physicians were slaves. Luke was faithful in writing about the life of Jesus and the Acts of the apostles in the early church. He was now with Paul in Rome. Even though Paul and Luke had not been to Colossae, the believers there would have been familiar with Luke. Luke was a well-educated man who was careful to write only what he could prove as true. His gospel is helpful in seeing the events of Jesus through the eyes of a Gentile. His writing of the Acts of the apostles he states came about because he wanted to give an accurate account of all that had happened after the departure of Jesus.

Demas also greets the church. Demas was with Paul when the letter was written to the Colossians. Later, he would forsake Paul, as Paul stated in Philemon: "Demas has forsaken me, loving this present world." We don't know much about Demas. He was a Gentile. We don't know when he came to be with Paul and don't know what caused him to leave. Paul says he loved the present world. Sadly, many who have followed Jesus for a time go away and do not return. One of my deacons used to say, "You are only saved for eternity if you are truly saved." Maybe Demas never got saved. Or maybe he was saved and walked away but was not lost. Eternal security is God's promises and only He knows who is saved and who is lost. While we may guess about Demas and others we have known, the truth is salvation is of the Lord, and only He knows who is saved and who is lost.

— *Lord, help me not to forsake You or Your workers.* —

> *Give my greetings to the brothers at Laodicea, and to Nympha and the church in her house. And when this letter has been read among you, have it also read in the church of the Laodiceans, and see that you also read the letter from Laodicea. (4:15-16)*

PAUL SAYS, "Give my greetings to the brothers at Laodicea." Epaphras had preached at Colossae, Laodicea and Hierapolis. At the time Paul wrote, these three cities were about the same size. Later, Laodicea would become more prominent than the other two. The church there was addressed by the apostle John and warned about having left their first love. Nympha was a woman who hosted a church in her home. The early church did not have buildings, and many of them met in the homes of the believers. Epaphras had probably told Paul about this church and Nympha. Many women in New Testament times were used by the Lord to help build and support the churches. We only have her name and know nothing else about her.

Paul instructs the believers that when the letter had been read among them to see that it was also read in the church of the Laodiceans. He also told them to read the letter from Laodicea. There is all kinds of speculations about the letter to the church at Laodicea. Some believe that it may be the same as the letter to the church at Ephesus. Tychicus had delivered both letters. But more than likely, his refers to a letter that was lost. Colossians and Ephesians were probably not written at the same time. And it is possible that Epaphras later brought the letter for Ephesus to Laodicea; that may not have happened. One thing we can know for sure: God preserved the letters He wanted in the Bible.

— *The Bible is the inerrant Word of God.* —

*And say to Archippus, "See that you fulfill the
ministry that you received in the Lord." (4:17)*

PAUL TELLS the believers at Colossae that they need to say to Archippus that he should fulfill the ministry he had received from the Lord. Archippus, whose name means "chief groom," was a member of the church at Colossae and eventually held some official position in the church. Some think that if Philemon was the host of the church at Colossae, maybe Archippus was the spiritual leader of the church. In Philemon verse 2, Paul calls Archippus a fellow soldier. Whatever the situation, it is clear that Paul wants Archippus to be encouraged by the believers at Colossae. It is a wonderful opportunity when any person has a responsibility in the church, and they need all the encouragement they can get. Being involved in any work of ministry is a blessing. Having those who encourage you is a real help in doing the work of ministry.

Paul wants the believers at Colossae to make sure they do all they can to help those in the ministry there. It is sometimes hard for ministry leaders to find the support and encouragement they need from those to whom they minister. What a wonderful blessing Archippus would have by being encouraged by the believers at Colossae. No doubt those believers would have told him that Paul was also encouraging him. Ministry is a shared work. The minister and the people work together to bring honor and glory to God. It is a real joy when the minister is encouraged and supported by the people that God has given him to lead. Paul wanted the believers at Colossae to help Archippus to stand against any false teachers that may come to the church. Truth is not to be compromised by anyone, especially those who lead. A church needs a man like Archippus to step up and fulfill his ministry.

— May we have leaders who stand for God's Word. —

> *I, Paul, write this greeting with my own hand.*
> *Remember my chains. Grace be with you. (4:18)*

IT WAS Paul's general practice to dictate his letters, but to write the closing sentences himself. Often, he did this to include some personal greetings, as he did here. Sometimes he signed his letters to help people know it really was his letter. Paul concluded this letter by sharing his heart about some of the workers and his hope for the continued work. He asks the church to remember his chains. Paul was not complaining about being in prison; he just wanted them to remember he was in prison. Paul believed that, even in prison, God was using him to further the gospel. All of Paul's labors had been to make Jesus Christ known to others. He had endured many hardships along his journey. Being in prison was not about to keep him from sharing Jesus. Even the guards understood that Paul was in prison for his faith.

Paul closes by saying, "Grace be with you." We must never forget that all we have is because of the grace of God. God so loved the world that He sent His Son. Had it not been for God's grace, we would never have had a way to God. Jesus stated, "I came to seek and to save the lost." That was Paul's mission. As he closes his letter, he once again reminds his readers of God's grace. The story is told of Dwight L. Moody walking in Chicago with one of his students. Toward them came a man who was obviously drunk. The student said to Moody, "Look at that poor drunk." Moody is said to have replied, "There but for the grace of God go I." None of us knows what we would be if not for the grace of God. Paul wants the church to know God's grace is with them. That same grace Paul shared with the believers at Colossae is ours today. May we be willing to share that grace with others.

— *Without Your grace, I would be lost. Thank You, Jesus.* —

CLOSING THOUGHTS

AS I WENT through Colossians, I was reminded once again that Jesus is Lord. That seems so obvious, but somehow we forget from time to time that He is indeed Lord. When we decide to go our own way or we decide to not do what we know God wants us to do, we are saying, "Not so, Lord." Our practical living must be founded on the fact that Jesus is Lord. He is Lord when it pleases me, and He is Lord when I am not so pleased about it. Some situations may cause us to question what the Lord is doing or what He is allowing to happen. But regardless of our circumstances, one truth remains: We can trust Him. The song writer said: "When you can't see His hand, trust His heart."

Paul wanted his readers to know Jesus Christ is the Supreme Lord of all. We need to surrender to Him and follow His leading. That is not always easy, but it is always necessary. We cannot live the Christian life by ourselves. The good news is we don't have to. God has given us His Spirit and His Word to teach us and to guide us. What we need to know, God will tell us. What we can't understand, we really don't need to know. Jesus said we must become as little children to enter the kingdom of God. Children trust what they are told and learn to obey what they are told.

As we grow in Christ, may we learn to trust and obey. We are the children of God. We need to begin to listen to the Father, and be obedient children. I hope you will remember that Jesus Christ is Lord of your life as you walk with Him.

Milton Keynes UK
Ingram Content Group UK Ltd.
UKHW021926281024
450365UK00017B/993